Shaun White

by Grace Hansen

OLYMPIC BIOGRAPHIES

Abdo Kids Jumbo is an Imprint of Abdo Kids
abdopublishing.com

abdopublishing.com

Published by Abdo Kids, a division of ABDO, P.O. Box 398166, Minneapolis, Minnesota 55439.
Copyright © 2019 by Abdo Consulting Group, Inc. International copyrights reserved in all countries.
No part of this book may be reproduced in any form without written permission from the publisher.
Abdo Kids Jumbo™ is a trademark and logo of Abdo Kids.

052018
092018

THIS BOOK CONTAINS
RECYCLED MATERIALS

Photo Credits: Alamy, AP Images, Getty Images, iStock, Shutterstock
Production Contributors: Teddy Borth, Jennie Forsberg, Grace Hansen
Design Contributors: Dorothy Toth, Laura Mitchell

Library of Congress Control Number: 2018936106
Publisher's Cataloging in Publication Data

Names: Hansen, Grace, author.
Title: Shaun White / by Grace Hansen.
Description: Minneapolis, Minnesota : Abdo Kids, 2019 | Series: Olympic
    biographies set 2 | Includes glossary, index and online resources (page 24).
Identifiers: ISBN 9781532181467 (lib. bdg.) | ISBN 9781532181566 (ebook) |
    ISBN 9781532181610 (Read-to-me ebook)
Subjects: LCSH: White, Shaun, 1986---Juvenile literature. | Olympic athletes--Juvenile literature. |
Winter Olympics--Juvenile literature. | Snowboarders--Juvenile literature.
 Classification: DDC 796.93092 [B]--dc23

Table of Contents

Early Years

Shaun White was born in San Diego, California, on September 3, 1986. He started snowboarding at the age of 6. He turned **pro** at 13 years old.

San Diego

Shaun competed in the 2003 Burton US Open. That year, he won the **slopestyle** event. At 16, he was the youngest person to win an Open event.

6

At the 2003 X Games in Aspen, Shaun won gold in **slopestyle** and **superpipe**. Today, he has earned a record 15 gold medals at the X Games. He is the only athlete to earn a perfect score on the superpipe.

8

From Snow to Skate

Later in 2003, Shaun turned

pro in skateboarding too!

He rode for Tony Hawk's

Birdhouse Skateboards.

Olympian

In 2006, Shaun joined team USA at his first Winter Olympics in Turin, Italy. Forty-four boarders competed in the men's **halfpipe**. Shaun won the gold!

13

Shaun joined team USA in 2010 at the Olympics in Vancouver. Again, he took home the gold in the **halfpipe**.

The 2014 Sochi Olympics was heartbreaking for Shaun. He came in fourth in the **halfpipe** event.

The 2018 Winter Olympics in South Korea was Shaun's time to shine. He had to beat Japan's Ayumu Hirano who had a score of 95.25.

In his final run, Shaun landed back-to-back **1440s**. He had never even practiced the combo move. He earned a score of 97.75 and the gold!

PyeongChang 2018

More Facts

- Shaun was born with a rare heart condition. He had to have three heart surgeries as a child to fix the problem.

- Shaun has had many nicknames over the years. When he was a kid, people called him "Future Boy" because they knew he'd do great things. He's also been called "The Flying Tomato."

- Shaun has talked about competing in the Tokyo Summer Games in 2020. He wants an Olympic gold medal in skateboarding!

Glossary

1440 – four full rotations.

halfpipe – an event where a snowboarder performs jumps and tricks on a snow-covered, U-shaped ramp.

pro – short for professional.

slopestyle – an event where a snowboarder moves down a course with a variety of obstacles including rails, jumps, and other terrain park features.

superpipe – an event in extreme sports where a snowboarder performs jumps and tricks on a snow-covered, U-shaped ramp that is larger than a regular halfpipe.

Index

Abdo Kids ONLINE
FREE! ONLINE MULTIMEDIA RESOURCES

Visit **abdokids.com** and use this code to access crafts, games, videos, and more!

Abdo Kids Code: OSK1467

24